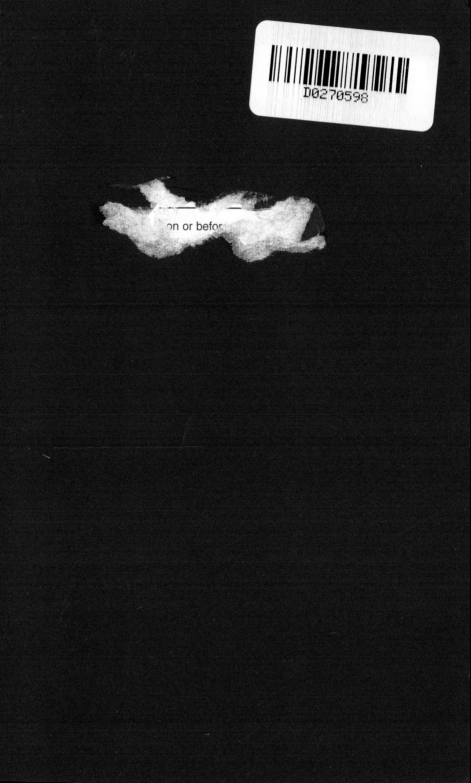

on or befor

Gallery Books
Editor: Peter Fallon

THE LONDON VERTIGO

Brian Friel

THE LONDON VERTIGO

Based on a play

THE TRUE BORN IRISHMAN

or

THE IRISH FINE LADY

by Charles Macklin

Gallery Books

The London Vertigo
is first published
simultaneously in paperback
and in a clothbound edition
in November 1990.

The Gallery Press
Loughcrew
Oldcastle
County Meath
Ireland

ISBN 1 85235 058 X (*paperback*)
    1 85235 059 8 (*clothbound*)

    The Gallery Press receives financial assistance from An Chomhairle Ealaíon / The Arts Council, Ireland, and acknowledges also the assistance of the Arts Council of Northern Ireland in the publication of this book.

for Owen, Emer and Chrissie

MacLochlainn's Vertigo

The desire to metamorphose oneself, to change everything utterly — name, beliefs, voice, loyalties, language, ambitions, even one's appearance — secretly excites most people at some stage of their lives and is as old as Adam. It is an element in the dream that charms young people into a career in acting. It is the private delirium that middle-aged writers are especially vulnerable to: to obliterate that whole past of botched and failed and embarrassing work and to begin afresh and anonymously with a few simple markings on a white sheet of paper. And of course the desire is a delusion. There are no new beginnings with new identities, as Cathal MacLochlainn, the eighteenth century actor and playwright, discovered. But his attempt at transmogrification is interesting for two reasons. The first is that he set about it with calculation and precocious acumen while he was still only a boy, long before he knew the pain of failure as a writer or as an actor. The second is that he pulled it off. Well, almost.

MacLochlainn was born some time during the last decade of the seventeenth century in the townland of Gortanarin in the parish of Cloncha in the Inishowen peninsula in the very north of County Donegal. Various birth-years are offered — 1690, 1693, 1699. Even as an old man (he died in 1797 when he may have been anything from ninety-eight to one hundred and seven) he never attempted to clear up the confusion, perhaps because the actor liked to be ageless, more likely because the writer preferred the past to be blurred. His background was poor peasant, his religion Catholicism, his only language Irish. Very early in life he recognised that an Irish-speaking Catholic peasant from north Donegal did not possess the very best qualifications for success in eighteenth century Ireland. He emigrated to England. He learned English and spoke it with an English accent. He changed his name to Charles Macklin. He invented a background of wealth and land in County Down. He converted to Protestantism. And the metamorphosis brought abundant success. London and Macklin loved one another. Before he was thirty he had a considerable reputation as a budding playwright and a rising star on the English stage. He became a friend of Garrick and Edmund Burke and Henry Fielding, was smiled on by royalty, was celebrated by Alexander Pope after the poet had seen his Shylock ('This is the Jew / That Shakespeare drew'), became famous for his Macbeth and his Iago and his own hugely popular *Love à la Mode*.

He was in his sixties when he wrote his first play with an Irish theme, *The True Born Irishman*, a satirical look at Irish Anglophiles; and one marvels at Macklin's ease and assurance in his new identity, so confident that he would now attempt to write out of a discarded persona. The play opened at the Crow Street theatre, Dublin, on May 14, 1761. Perhaps predictably Irish audiences received it warmly.

The plot is simple. Nancy O'Doherty, wife of Murrough O'Doherty (played by Macklin himself), a pompous and ponderous Dublin burgher, has been to London for the coronation of George the Third. During her brief visit she has been smitten by 'the London vertigo', a sudden and dizzy conviction that London is the very heart of style and wit and good fortune and excitement. When the play opens she has recently returned to dreary Murrough O'Doherty.

Macklin wants her to be an absurd and ludicrous figure. He achieves this — without a hint of irony, it would seem — by two devices: the lady, now ashamed of her Irish name, O'Doherty, has decided to call herself Mrs Diggerty; and she now speaks a patois in a posh accent that her husband can scarcely understand. 'London — Dublin — don't neem them together!' she says. 'After London everything I set my eyes on here gives me the *ennui* and the *contre cure*. The streets are mean, the houses dirty, the people ridiculous. And the women! None of the *non chalance*, none of that *jenny-see-quee* we have in London. And everything sounds so strange here! Even the very dogs when they bark, I swear they bark wit' a brogue!'

O'Doherty, distressed by his wife's lunacy, enlists the help of her brother and together they hatch a plot to restore her to sanity and thorough Irishness. By a series of complicated and cruel manoeuvres Macklin has Mrs Diggerty cured of her vertigo, properly humiliated before her friends and reconciled to decent Dublin domesticity. Simultaneously and almost certainly unwittingly Macklin has written his own biography as comedy/farce.

Six years passed before he brought *The True Born Irishman* to London. It opened in Covent Garden on November 28, 1767. Circumspect as ever, Macklin retitled the play *The Irish Fine Lady* just in case the original title might have a hint of coat-trailing for his English audience. But the play did not travel. Whatever the reason the night was a disaster. And when the curtain came down Macklin rushed on to the stage in panic. 'Ladies and gentlemen,' he pleaded, 'I am very sensible that there are several passages in this play which deserve to be reprobated and I assure you that they shall never offend your ears again.' One can almost hear the terrified voice and the clipped Donegal vowels. Later, when he had composed himself, he said to a friend, 'I believe the audience are right. There is a geography in humour as well as in morals, which I had previously not considered.' What he meant by a geography in humour is clear enough; a geography in morals is nicely ambiguous. Anyhow *The Irish Fine Lady* was withdrawn after that one performance.

I have worked on Macklin's text with affection and respect. I have pruned his script vigorously, mainly by compressing his three acts into one and by reducing his cast of fourteen to a cast of five. (The missing nine appear only briefly in his Act 2 and Act 3 and he uses them not to energise his central theme but as contemporary stereotypes who make leisurely and amusing social comment on mid-eighteenth century Ireland; in other words to stroke his audience.) But I trust — I believe — I have done neither structural nor aesthetic damage to the script. And in excuse for my ruthless culling of his cast I plead the stern economics of late twentieth century theatre. Indeed my hope is that a lean and less discursive text may be more attractive to theatre companies today and better suited to our impatient stage.

My reason for renaming the play *The London Vertigo* is that this title both signposts the play's theme and hints at the fate the author himself so eagerly embraced.

This may not be Macklin's best play — *The Man of the World* or *Love à la Mode* claims that place. But it is a very considerable piece of work from an almost completely self-made man and it gave me pleasure to work on it — a kind of *comhar* or cooperation or companionship with a neighbouring playwright.

Brian Friel

Characters

MURROUGH O'DOHERTY, self-assured Dublin burgher
KATTY FARREL, family servant
TOM HAMILTON, slow-thinking and pompous lawyer
MRS DIGGERTY, O'Doherty's wife
COUNT MUSHROOM, typical 18th century fop, stage-English in
   accent and manner

Time: an afternoon and evening in September 1761.
Place: the drawing-room in Murrough O'Doherty's Dublin
home.

MURROUGH O'DOHERTY *is dozing on a chair, an open book on his lap. Enter* KATTY FARREL, *the maid.*

KATTY   Mr O'Doherty, sir. Mr O'Doherty.

O'DOHERTY   Mm? Mm? Yes? What is it?

KATTY   Your brother-in-law gives his compliments to you, Mr O'Doherty.

O'DOHERTY   Yes, Katty? Yes? Yes?

KATTY   Counsellor Hamilton, the barrister.

O'DOHERTY   Yes?

KATTY   He gives his compliments to you, sir.

O'DOHERTY   Splendid, Katty. Thank you.

KATTY   He's on his way upstairs.

O'DOHERTY   What's that you have in your hand?

KATTY   A card for my mistress — From Madam Mulrooney.

O'DOHERTY   Pray let me see it. 'Mrs Mulrooney makes her compliments to Mrs Murrough O'Doherty and likewise to Mr Murrough O'Doherty and hopes to have the favour of their company on Sunday 17th instant to play at cards, sup and spend the evening with Count Mushroom, Lady Kinnegad, Lord Ballybeg, Captain Kilmaine, Major Bellaghy, Lady Belmullet — ' Here, Katty. Take this to your mistress. I have nothing to say to it.

KATTY   Very well, Mr O'Doherty.

She exits.

O'DOHERTY   (*To audience*) Mrs Mulrooney! She's another of the fine ladies of this country who, like my wife, is sending her soul to the devil and her husband to jail as fast as she can. Mr Mulrooney, the boob, has scarce a thousand pounds a year in the world; yet he spends above two thousand in equipage — in other words on a carriage and servants — on jolly parties and high living besides what his fool of a wife loses to that female-sharper, my Lady

Kinnegad; which, if I may judge by my own wife, is at least a good two thousand more; so that by the rule of subtraction, take four thousand pounds a year out of one thousand pounds and in a very little time nothing will remain but the jail — or a fast packet boat to France. Money! Money! They think it grows on trees, these women!

Enter COUNSELLOR HAMILTON.

HAMILTON Murrough! I'm extremely glad to see you.
O'DOHERTY By my faith and so am I you, too, Tom. You are most welcome, brother-in-law. Odzooks, give us a kiss, man.

They embrace.

O'DOHERTY I give you my honour I am as glad to see you in Dublin at this juncture as I should to see a hundred head of fat bullocks upon my own land all ready for Ballinasloe fair.
HAMILTON That is a great compliment from you, brother. (*To audience*) Fat bullock — curious image.
O'DOHERTY A very true compliment, I assure you. (*To audience*) All beef — no brains.
HAMILTON And I see by the newspapers that my sister is returned from the coronation frolics.
O'DOHERTY (*To audience*) George III.
HAMILTON (*To audience*) September 22, 1761.
O'DOHERTY (*To audience*) London.
HAMILTON (*To audience*) England.
O'DOHERTY
HAMILTON } (*To audience*) God bless His Majesty.
O'DOHERTY She has returned with a vengeance.
HAMILTON What's the matter?
O'DOHERTY Returned with a distemper that will soon affect the whole nation. It is called the Irish Fine Lady's Delirium — or the London Vertigo.
HAMILTON What may that be?

O'DOHERTY The devil an inhabitant in Jonathan Swift's Hospital for Lunatics is in a worse pickle than she is.

HAMILTON (*To audience*) Opened here in Dublin four years ago.

> 'He gave the little wealth he had
> To found a house for fools and mad.'

O'DOHERTY If you were to hear her when the fit is upon her — oh, she is as mad — the devil a thing in this poor country but what gives her the spleen and the vapours. Then such a frenzy of admiration for everything in England! And among the rest of her madness she has brought back — (*He looks around and lowers his voice*) — a new language with her.

HAMILTON A new — ?

O'DOHERTY A new kind of London English that is no more like our Irish English than — than — than a fine gilded carriage is like a Carrickmore cart. What name do you think she went by when she was in England?

HAMILTON What do you mean?

O'DOHERTY What did she call herself over there?

HAMILTON What would she call herself but Nancy O'Doherty!

O'DOHERTY O'Doherty! Oho! Upon my honour, Tom, she startles when she hears the name O'Doherty, and blushes, and is much ashamed as if a man said something bawdy to her. No, no, my friend; my wife, your sister is no longer the plain, modest, good-natured, domestic, obedient Irish Mrs O'Doherty — in other words the perfect wife; but the travelled, rampant, high-lifed, prancing, English ... Mrs Diggerty.

HAMILTON Diggerty?

O'DOHERTY Diggerty. Was there ever such impertinence? Nor is that all of your sister's whims and madnesses.

HAMILTON There is more?

O'DOHERTY She wants me to go after a title. Can you imagine! Young Lord Turnabout has hinted to her that if I throw my weight behind him in the coming election a title is mine for the asking. And that piece of information has stirred up such a rage of quality and title in her giddy head that I cannot rest night or day for her importunity!

HAMILTON Good heavens!

O'DOHERTY She would have me desert my friends and sell myself, my honour and my country, as several others have done before me, so that she may sink the ancient name of O'Doherty in the upstart title of Lady Ahohill or Lady Culmore or some such ridiculous nonsense.

HAMILTON (*To audience*) 'Sell my country'! He really means it would cost him money!

O'DOHERTY Oh Tom, Tom, I have many grievances to tell you of but I have one that is even more whimsical than all the rest.

HAMILTON Tell me.

O'DOHERTY I am going to be a cuckold.

HAMILTON My sister? — Your wife? — You mean she is going to — ?

O'DOHERTY There is an English coxcomb just arrived among us in this town who thinks every woman that sees him is in love with him.

HAMILTON Who is this spark?

O'DOHERTY His name is Mushroom, as in . . . mushroom. Maurice Mushroom. Count Maurice Mushroom.

HAMILTON And he lives here, this cuckold-maker?

O'DOHERTY You know those huge estates owned by Lord Oldcastle?

HAMILTON On which your family for generations have had long and very profitable leases?

O'DOHERTY The same. (*To audience*) Is the boob getting saucy?

HAMILTON And have sublet at enormous profit to much less fortunate Irishmen?

O'DOHERTY (*To audience*) Indeed he is! (*To* HAMILTON) Well, my Lord Oldcastle has made this Mushroom his agent in this country and sent him over to settle his affairs here. Now one of the main businesses he must conclude is an agreement between Oldcastle and me on the terms of the leases; and Mushroom and I not being able to agree on the terms, what does the coxcomb do?

Pause.

HAMILTON You and he disagree.

O'DOHERTY (*To audience*) Noodle-brain! (*To* HAMILTON) What he does is this, Tom. He sends my wife a warm billet-doux in which he very gallantly tells her that *she* shall settle the leases at her own price — only upon the trifling condition that he may be permitted now and again to be the occasional lord of her ladyship's matrimonial manor.

HAMILTON So he just wants occasional lodgings here, Murrough?

O'DOHERTY In a manner of speaking — yes. (*To audience*) Close to genius, wouldn't you say?

HAMILTON That is trifling indeed.

O'DOHERTY Do you think so? (*To audience*) Himself — his sister — all the Hamiltons — mahogany heads!

HAMILTON And pray, what says my sister to all this?

O'DOHERTY She knows nothing of it.

HAMILTON But she got Mushroom's letter, did she not?

O'DOHERTY I intercepted it — with the help of Katty Farrel. And with Katty's assistance I have carried on a correspondence with the fellow in my wife's name — unknown to her, of course. And by that means I shall not only detect and expose the fellow but get an excellent bargain of the leases which are to be signed this very day!

HAMILTON But, Murrough, you couldn't accept the leases upon those terms.

O'DOHERTY   Could I not? (*To audience*) And he's a barrister!
Question is: How did the noodle ever qualify?

HAMILTON   (*To audience*) Forging letters in my sister's
name! Lord Counterfeit!

O'DOHERTY   (*To audience*) Of course he'd make a living
nowhere else but at the law.

HAMILTON   (*To audience*) And involving decent Katty
Farrel in his corruption! No wonder our Mama
always hated him!

Enter KATTY.

KATTY   Sir, Count Mushroom is below.

She exits.

O'DOHERTY   I will wait upon him, Katty. Now, brother, you
shall see one of the pertest and most conceited impudent coxcombs that has ever been
imported into this land or that disgraced
humanity.

MUSHROOM   (*Off*) My compliments to your lady, Mrs Katty.
I will be with her in the twinkling of a star —

O'DOHERTY   D'you hear?

MUSHROOM   — or in less time than a single glance of her
own immortal beauty can pass to the centre of
an amorous heart.

O'DOHERTY   (*Eyes closed*) Control, Murrough O'Doherty!
Control!

Enter MUSHROOM.

MUSHROOM   My dear Diggerty, I kiss your hand. I am come
on purpose to discuss the leases that you and I
— (*He sees* HAMILTON) I beg ten thousand
pardons — I see you are busy —

O'DOHERTY   Indeed, Count, we are not. Tom Hamilton, my
wife's brother — Count Mushroom.

MUSHROOM   Sir, I feel a superlative happiness in being
known to you. I have long expected and long

wished for it with a lover's appetite. Therefore, without waiting for the dull advocation of experience or the pedantic forms of ceremony, I beg you will honour me with a niche in your esteem and register me in the select catalogue of your most constant and most ardent friends and admirers.

Pause.

HAMILTON   That's right.

O'DOHERTY   (*To audience*) And he'll be a judge some day!

MUSHROOM   Give me your hand, Hamilton. It's Tom, isn't it? Yes, it's Tom. Give me your hand, dear Tom Hamilton. You are Diggerty's friend. Diggerty is your friend. Diggerty is my friend. I am Diggerty's friend. So it follows that you and I are destined to be friends since friends of friends must naturally be friends, too. But that's enough. I'll serve you. Say no more. I'll serve you. Rely upon me, friend.

HAMILTON   You live in this town, Count?

MUSHROOM   Quite *en famille*. I go about everywhere, am of no party but those of love, pleasure and gallantry. The women like me and commend me at cards, tea, scandal and dancing. The men commend me at jolly parties, a late hour, a bottle and hazard —

HAMILTON   (*To audience*) 'Hazard' — in other words, dice. You know, a small cube having its faces marked with spots numbering from —

O'DOHERTY   They know — they know!

MUSHROOM   I love ease, hate ceremony and am at home wherever I go. Correct, Diggerty?

O'DOHERTY   To give you your due, Count, you are never bashful in any place.

MUSHROOM   Bashfulness, dear Diggerty, is a mask of ignorance, a disease of the vulgar and uncourtly — what we men of the world are never infected with. But to business, my friend.

O'DOHERTY Business?

MUSHROOM The leases, Diggerty. Lord Oldcastle's leases.

O'DOHERTY Of course.

MUSHROOM Cards on the table, my friend: My lord is loath
to lose you as a tenant just as I am convinced it
would be for his interest you should have the
lands. So let us sign and seal at once — upon
your own terms. For really I think tenants in
Ireland want encouragement; they are racked
too high; they are indeed; it is a shame they
should be racked so high. (*To* HAMILTON) You
want encouragement in trade, too — tax
concessions — greater incentives — relief in
exports — that sort of thing. I'll speak to some
people of consequence about it — on the other
side.

HAMILTON On the other side of what?

O'DOHERTY London, Tom, London.

HAMILTON Ah. (*To* MUSHROOM) Will you?

MUSHROOM Upon my honour. The moment I return.

O'DOHERTY You English politicians promise us the devil
and all while you are among us. But the
moment you get to the other side you have
devilish bad memories.

HAMILTON You seem to like Ireland, sir?

MUSHROOM A damn fine country, Tom. Upon the whole,
take you all together, you are a damned honest
tory rory, rantum scantum, dancing, singing,
laughing, boozing, jolly, friendly, fighting,
hospitable people. And I like you mightily.

O'DOHERTY (*To audience*) Nothing changes, does it?

MUSHROOM I do upon honour and I believe I shall marry
one of your women here, grow domestic and
settle among you. But I beg pardon, my dear
Diggerty. I must rob you of my company for a
moment to pay my duty to your lady. (*Catches*
HAMILTON's *hand*) Hamilton — yours, yours.
Give me thy hand, Diggerty. (*To* O'DOHERTY)
From this moment set me down as thy unalter-
able friend. I'll serve you — rely upon me — I'll

serve you.

He moves towards the door and pauses there.

MUSHROOM (*To audience*) And now to try my hand at casual lodgings — bed and perhaps board?

He exits. KATTY *enters.*

O'DOHERTY Didn't I tell you? There never was so conceited and so impudent a coxcomb as that puppy! (*To* KATTY) Is your fine mistress dressed yet, Katty?

KATTY The mistress, sir — she — she — (*Uneasy in front of* HAMILTON) — she has had a little misfortune, sir.

O'DOHERTY Speak up, Katty. No secrets here.

KATTY You know that bill that came from Covent Garden, from the mercer there?

HAMILTON (*To audience*) In other words, draper.

O'DOHERTY I gave her the money for that two days ago, Katty.

KATTY Lost it all last night — to Lady Kinnegad.

O'DOHERTY My God! All?

KATTY Playing brag.

O'DOHERTY (*To audience*) A kind of poker that's played with — (*Recovering. To* KATTY) She played brag with that sharper?

KATTY And to cover up her excesses she's going to borrow from Count Mushroom.

O'DOHERTY And what collateral has she to — (*We hear* MUSHROOM *and* MRS DIGGERTY *laugh off*) Don't answer that!

HAMILTON Oh, Murrough, the woman has lost all sense of shame.

O'DOHERTY She is not to borrow from Mushroom, Katty. Here — here — here — give her this. Say you borrowed it from your brother — from a friend — say you —

Enter MUSHROOM *and* MRS DIGGERTY. *She is*

gaudily dressed and, as Macklin says, 'What a head she has!' — i.e. extravagantly dressed hair.

O'DOHERTY   Ah, my dear.

MRS DIGGERTY   Brother, I am veestly glad to see you.

HAMILTON   Welcome home from England, Nancy.

MRS DIGGERTY   I am imminsely obligated to you, brother.

HAMILTON   Did it answer your expectations?

MRS DIGGERTY   Ravishingly.

HAMILTON   Indeed?

MRS DIGGERTY   Transcendently.

HAMILTON   I'm glad you —

MRS DIGGERTY   Beyond all degrees of compirison. England, brother, England is just veest, imminse, extatic! I never knew life before. Everything there is high, tip top, the *grand monde*, the bun tun —

HAMILTON   (*To audience*) Bun tun?

MRS DIGGERTY   — and quite, quite teesty.

MUSHROOM   She liked it.

HAMILTON   And London?

MRS DIGGERTY   London? The place of the world, brother!

HAMILTON   Then this town, I suppose, is —

MRS DIGGERTY   This town? Where? Where? — I've forgot — what's the neem of this place?

O'DOHERTY   Dublin.

MRS DIGGERTY   Dublin! That's it! Oh dear brother, London — Dublin — don't neem them together. After London everything I set my eyes on here gives me the *ennui* and the *contre cure*. The streets are mean, the houses dirty, the people ridiculous. And the women! None of the *non chalance*, none of that *jenny-see-quee* we have in London. And everything sounds so strange here; everybody talks so peculiar; I scarcely understand them. Even the very dogs when they bark, I swear they bark wit' a brogue.

O'DOHERTY   As strong a brogue as your mother, Madge Gallagher from Donegal Town, ever had.

MRS DIGGERTY	You are a very rude man to remind me of my mother's family. You know I always despised my mother's family. Didn't I, brother? I hate the very neem of — What was my mother's maiden name?
HAMILTON	Gallagher.
MRS DIGGERTY	That's it. Gillogher. Hate it. Hate it.
HAMILTON	Tell us about the coronation, sister. No doubt you were there?
MRS DIGGERTY	There? O *moundew* — what a quistion! Ax the Count.
MUSHROOM	She was everywhere — and with everybody. The court never stirred without her.
MRS DIGGERTY	But the highlight of the visit was the feast in the Guildhall. That — was — just — imminse! I went to it with her grace, a friend of mine, and a peerty of the court, as one of the household. And the moment I entered that imminse hall every eye was upon me! So this is the handsome Irishwoman — the famous Irish toast — the celebrated Mrs Diggerty! I was just brilliant, even more brilliant than I was at the coronation itself. I was so brilliant that night at the coronation ball that the count was moved to write a poem about me.
MUSHROOM	Oh heavens, madam!
MRS DIGGERTY	It's true. And he is one of the prettiest poets we have in England or for that matter in — in — in — what's the name of this — ?
O'DOHERTY	Ireland.
MRS DIGGERTY	Ireland — that's it! He is by my honour.
HAMILTON	I don't doubt the gentleman's talents in the least, sister.
MUSHROOM	You are most polite, sir, and the lady is pleased to rally.
O'DOHERTY	(*To audience*) In other words — to banter.
MUSHROOM	My muse is but a smatterer, a slattern, a mere slip-shod lady.
MRS DIGGERTY	What I say is true. And to convince you of his worth — (*She produces a paper from her bosom*)

	— will you be so obliging as to read them to my brother?
MUSHROOM	The nod of beauty sways both gods and men and I obey. Gentlemen, the title will at once let you into the whole of what you are to expect in this little production: *An Extempore On The Famous Mrs Diggerty Dancing At Court.*
MRS DIGGERTY	La la loo.
O'DOHERTY	(*To audience*) Oh God.
MUSHROOM	Now attend.

<blockquote>
'When beauteous Diggerty leads up the dance
In fair Britannia's court,
Then every heart is in a prance
And longs for Cupid's sport.'
</blockquote>

MRS DIGGERTY	'Cupid's sport'! Naughty — naughty!
MUSHROOM	<blockquote>'Beaux ogle and pant and gaze; Belles envy and sneer, yet praise, As Venus herself were there — '</blockquote>
MRS DIGGERTY	'Venus'! Oh, Count!
MUSHROOM	'And prudes agree it must be she — '
MRS DIGGERTY	It must be Venus herself.
MUSHROOM	<blockquote>'It must be she — or Diggerty. It must be she — or Diggerty, Or Diggerty, the fair.'</blockquote>

He bows very low to MRS DIGGERTY. *Enter* KATTY.

	That's it, gentlemen; a slight effort of the muse; a mere *jeu d'esprit.*
KATTY	My Lady Kinnegad and my Lady Belmullet have arrived, Mrs O'Doherty.
MRS DIGGERTY	Who is that creature addressing? Nobody of that neem here, my dear.
O'DOHERTY	(*Angrily*) I want to sign those leases now, Count. Now! I'll await you downstairs. Come with me, Katty. I want a word with you.

He goes off.

MUSHROOM	With all my heart, Diggerty.
MRS DIGGERTY	You'll return later this evening, Count, won't you? I'm having some titled friends in for cards.
MUSHROOM	Do I breathe? Do I exist? I will but step down, sign the papers and return tonight on the wings of inclination, *ma chère belle sans adieu.*

Exits.

MRS DIGGERTY	*Au revoir.* 'Then every heart is in a prance' — isn't he the most humorous creature, Tom?
HAMILTON	Most.
MRS DIGGERTY	And mighty witty — don't you think so?
HAMILTON	Mighty.
MRS DIGGERTY	'And longs for Cupid's sport.' And so do I! Oh brother, brother, you are looking at a transported woman! *Adieu.*

She rushes off. HAMILTON *is totally bewildered. He stares at the audience for several seconds before he speaks.*

HAMILTON	Compared with her the inhabitants of Swift's Hospital for Lunatics are marvellously sane. Oh the poor woman, she is very far gone and must be pinched to the quick — and shall this very night. Thank heaven our Mama has passed on.

He goes to the door, stops, turns and addresses the audience again.

Bun tun — tory rory — rantum scantum — what do those words mean? Must ask Mirragh — O'Duggerty — O'Murragh — O'Diggerty — Oh God —

He dashes off.
A short time later. The stage is in darkness.

Then KATTY *enters and lights candles. Now we hear* O'DOHERTY *and his wife arguing off.*

MRS DIGGERTY (*Off*) Reason? Reason? I will have no reason, Mr Diggerty! There can be no reason against what I say! You are the strangest man — not to be a lord! I insist upon it, sir! There is a necessity for a peerage!

KATTY *exits.*

O'DOHERTY Show me the necessity then and all my objections will vanish.

MRS DIGGERTY Why, sir, I am affronted for want of a title. (*They both enter*) A parcel of upstarts with their crownets upon their coaches, their chairs, their spoons, their handkerchiefs, nay on their very knockers — (*To audience*) in other words on their doors — (*To O'Doherty*) creatures that were below me but t'other day are now truly my superiors and have their precedency and are set above me at table.

O'DOHERTY Come, come, my dear. Don't be in such a fluster.

MRS DIGGERTY Can there be anything more provoking to a woman of my teest and spirit than to hear the titles of these ugly creatures bawled in one's ear upon every occasion: 'My Lady Kinnegad's coach here'; 'My Lady Belmullet's chair there'; 'My Lady Ahohil's chariot here'. And what are they all? Upstarts! With Upstart titles! And then consider how vile my neem sounds: 'Mrs Diggerty's servants here'; 'Mrs Diggerty's chair there'; 'Mrs Diggerty's coach here'. It's mean. It's beggarly. I can't bear it. The very thought of it makes me ready to burst my stays and almost throws me into hysteria.

She flings herself on the couch and howls.

O'DOHERTY   Now, now, my dear, don't work yourself up
            into a fit.
MRS DIGGERTY   My life is miserable. (*Rises*) But I see your
            design: you have a mind to break my heart.
            (*Howls*) Yes, you argue and contradict me for
            no other end; you do everything to fret and vex
            me.
O'DOHERTY   What does that mean?
MRS DIGGERTY   Ever since I returned from England to this —
            this — this —
O'DOHERTY   Ireland.
MRS DIGGERTY   That's the odious neem. Ever since my un-
            happy return I have been requesting, begging,
            praying that you would send to London for a
            set of long-tailed horses that you know I
            admire so much.
O'DOHERTY   Have you any idea of the cost of — !
MRS DIGGERTY   Lady Ballybeg has a set. Lady Kilmaine has a
            set. Lady Newry has a set. You know very well
            I detest a short tail. (*To audience*) Don't we all?
            Every lady of figure loves long tails. Nobody
            but doctors, lawyers and country merchants
            have short tails now.
O'DOHERTY   Very well, my dear, very well. You will have
            tails as long as Lord Newry or Lord Ballybeg or
            whoever. As to the title, if it can be had —
MRS DIGGERTY   You know it can be had! Just open your tight
            purse! Let me hear no more about it — for a
            title I will have. I can't bear being plain Mrs
            Diggerty any longer.

            *Again she howls and throws herself on the
            couch. Enter* KATTY.

KATTY   Is Mrs O'Doherty ill, sir?
O'DOHERTY   Very ill — with distemper.

            He takes KATTY *aside.*

            Well, Katty?

KATTY Everything's in hand, sir.

O'DOHERTY The house is empty?

KATTY Yes, sir.

O'DOHERTY Her card friends all gone?

KATTY Everybody's left, sir. They promise to return in an hour.

O'DOHERTY Good. And Mushroom?

KATTY He got out of his carriage at the gate and crept back to the house.

O'DOHERTY Where is he now?

KATTY In the back parlour. Dressing himself in my lady's clothes.

O'DOHERTY That you provided.

KATTY On your instructions, sir.

O'DOHERTY Shhh! I know. I know. How did you persuade him?

KATTY I told him, if he were sighted, he would pass as a laundry woman. (*She laughs*)

O'DOHERTY Shhh!

KATTY You never saw a man — a woman — so eager, sir.

O'DOHERTY Please, Katty.

KATTY Bursting with expectation — in a manner of speaking.

O'DOHERTY Katty, please.

KATTY He's ten times fonder of himself as a woman than he was as a man — if that's possible.

O'DOHERTY I will cure him of his passion for himself and for all Irish women as long as he lives. Here comes her brother. Let us get out of their way for he is resolved to startle the lady and waken her — if possible. They will have a very sharp brush, I reckon. Mushroom's turn comes later.

They exit. HAMILTON *enters.*

HAMILTON Sit up and pay attention to me, Nancy. (*To audience*) Brothers sometimes have stern duties to perform. Sister, I have words for you.

MRS DIGGERTY Can't you see I'm in no state to — ?

HAMILTON   Immediately, madam! This very instant! You are not ignorant that your husband took you without a fortune. You know, too, that by the marriage articles, upon a separation or your husband's death, you are entitled to only £100 a year. Now, madam, I am commissioned to inform you that the doors are open and that the stipulated sum will be paid punctually —

MRS DIGGERTY   You're not — ?

HAMILTON   For know that neither your husband's love, my affection, nor a residence in this house can be enjoyed by you another hour — but on the hard condition of a thorough reformation.

MRS DIGGERTY   You're telling me I must — ?

HAMILTON   If female vanity will be mad, husbands must be peremptory. (*To audience*) I used that line in court once. The judge commended it. (*To* MRS DIGGERTY) The sums of money you have squandered and those you have been cheated of by your female friends — that is the least offence in your husband's judgement. It is your pride, your midnight revels, insolence of taste, rage of precedency that grieve him; for they have made you the ridicule of every flirt and coxcomb, and the scorn and pity of every sober person that knows your folly. This reflects disgrace upon your friends, contempt upon the spirit and credit of your husband and has furnished whispering suspicion with stories and implications which have secretly fixed an infectious stain upon your chastity.

She jumps to her feet.

MRS DIGGERTY   My chastity? I defy the world! I care not what slander says! I will rely upon my innocence! (*To audience*) That was a bit hasty, wasn't it?

HAMILTON   It is not sufficient to rely on innocence alone, madam. Women must not only be innocent, they must appear so, too. (*To audience*) This play was written over two hundred years ago. Times — unfortunately — have changed.

MRS DIGGERTY I don't know what you mean by all this, brother. I beg you will explain.

HAMILTON I will. Know, then, that the coxcomb Mushroom —

MRS DIGGERTY Mushroom?

HAMILTON — took some hints your liberty had given him —

MRS DIGGERTY I gave him hints? Brother, you — !

HAMILTON — and like a true man of intrigue not only returns your hints with a letter of gallantry but bribes your own woman to deliver it.

MRS DIGGERTY Katty? I will turn her out — !

HAMILTON But the maid, instead of carrying the letter to you, delivers that and many others to her master —

MRS DIGGERTY To dear Murrough? (*To audience*) The bitch!

HAMILTON — who in your name, hand, style and sentiment has answered them all and carried on an amorous correspondence with the gentleman —

MRS DIGGERTY Mushroom?

HAMILTON — even up to an assignation. And now at this very instant the spark is preparing for that happy interview.

MRS DIGGERTY With my husband? Tom, I — !

HAMILTON With you, sister. Not only that but he has made the whole town confident of his good fortune.

MRS DIGGERTY Oh Lord!

HAMILTON Now judge what your husband, your brother and your friends must think of her whose conduct could entitle a coxcomb to such liberties.

MRS DIGGERTY I shall make no defence, brother. The story shocks me. Help me. Advise me. (*To audience*) Well, I'm caught, amn't I? (*To* HAMILTON) Only say what I shall do to be revenged upon this fellow for his impudence and what will convince my husband and you, Tom, and all

	the world of my innocence — and I will do it. Oh, Tom, you have given such a stirring to my heart and such a trouble and trembling as it never felt before.
HAMILTON	It is the stirring of virtue, sister.
MRS DIGGERTY	Is it?
HAMILTON	Encourage it.
MRS DIGGERTY	I will — I will.
HAMILTON	For tears of repentance are the brightest ornaments a modern fine lady can be decked in.
MRS DIGGERTY	(*To audience*) Wouldn't he give you an ache in the jerkin?
O'DOHERTY	(*Off*) I shall be in here, Katty. The moment he makes a move, bring me word.
KATTY	(*Off*) I shall, sir.
MRS DIGGERTY	It's Mr Diggerty. Oh, brother, I am ashamed to face him.

Enter O'DOHERTY.

O'DOHERTY	Well, Tom, have you spoken to her?
HAMILTON	There she is, sir, bathed in tears of humility and repentance, as she should be.

MRS DIGGERTY *howls.*

O'DOHERTY	Oh, you've gone too far, brother. You shouldn't have made her cry. Nancy, child, turn round and don't be crying there.
MRS DIGGERTY	I'm ashamed to look you in the face, sir. (*Howls*)
O'DOHERTY	Had I been here, brother, I assure you you should not have made her cry.
MRS DIGGERTY	My errors I acknowledge — (*Howls*)
O'DOHERTY	Nancy —
MRS DIGGERTY	— and for the future it will be the business of my life to — to — to — (*Howls*)
O'DOHERTY	No more — not another word — no more. If you have settled everything with your brother, that is sufficient. Turn round and give me a

	kiss. Let us be friends at once. (*They kiss*) There. In that kiss now let all tears and uneasiness subside in you as all fears and resentment shall die in me.
HAMILTON	I must have my kiss of peace, too. (*They kiss*) I own I have been a little severe with you but your disease did require sharp medicine.
O'DOHERTY	Now, Nancy, I have a favour or two to beg of you.
MRS DIGGERTY	Command them, Murrough.
O'DOHERTY	The first thing I ask is that you sack that French cook and let us have the food that every ordinary Irishman has.
MRS DIGGERTY	He goes tomorrow. (*To audience*) Back to the frying-pan.
O'DOHERTY	Then let us be rid of your London English with your neems and your teestys and your veestlys and your imminselys.
MRS DIGGERTY	They're dispinsed with — dispensed with now.
O'DOHERTY	And above all things, pray never again call me Diggerty. My name is Murrough O'Doherty and I am not ashamed of it. But that damned name Diggerty, my dear it — it — it dements me.
MRS DIGGERTY	Then upon my honour, Murrough O'Doherty, you'll never be demented again.

Enter KATTY.

	(*To audience*) That wasn't too bad after all — was it?
KATTY	Mr Mushroom is on his way up, sir.
O'DOHERTY	In my lady's clothes?
MRS DIGGERTY	What's this?
KATTY	Yes, sir.
MRS DIGGERTY	Mushroom? — In my clothes?
KATTY	And looking very pretty, madam.
MRS DIGGERTY	(*To* O'DOHERTY) Has he gone suddenly — soufflé?

36

O'DOHERTY Gone what?

MRS DIGGERTY You know — (*She gestures*) — *soufflé*.

HAMILTON (*To audience*) In other words — made fluffy with beaten egg whites and then heated in an oven until it puffs up.

O'DOHERTY Mushroom? Not that toadstool! Detain him for a moment, Katty.

KATTY leaves.

Go to your room. I'll come and instruct you how to behave.

MRS DIGGERTY Anything to be avenged on that — that pup!

She exits.

O'DOHERTY Leave me with him, Tom. We mustn't prevent that man from making me a cuckold.

HAMILTON Be sure you make the gentleman smart.

Exits.

O'DOHERTY (*To audience*) I'll make him smart. And smarter. Impudent rascal — to make a cuckold of an Irishman — take our own trade out of our own hands! And a branch of business we pride ourselves so much in, too. Why, sure that and the manufacture of linen are the only free trades we have. (*Moves to door. Stops*) 'Soufflé' — never heard that term before. Must be a London usage. (*Moves again. Stops*) Where would she have heard it? Damn.

He hears KATTY and MUSHROOM off and quickly exits.

KATTY (*Off*) I protest I should not have known you, sir.

MUSHROOM (*Off*) Don't you think I make a handsome woman, Mrs Katty?

They are now both on.

KATTY   You are a perfect beauty, sir — madam. I'll go and see if the coast is clear and tell my mistress you are come.

MUSHROOM   Tell her my soul is all rapture, ecstasy and transport and rides upon the wings of love.

KATTY *exits.*

(*To audience*) A man must speak nonsense to these creatures or they will not believe he loves them. Trouble is — *all* these Irish women love me. I'll have more intrigues in this country than I shall know what to do with. Old Diggerty here, when I tire of her, I'll bring her across to England and bequeath her to my Lord Oldcastle. (*To* MRS DIGGERTY *and* KATTY *who have entered*) My angel! My goddess!

MRS DIGGERTY   It's not — is it? — Count Mushroom?

MUSHROOM   The same. All aquiver. Oh my delight —

MRS DIGGERTY   But if my husband should discover you —

MUSHROOM   Love despises all dangers when such beauty as yours is the price. (*To* KATTY) See we're not distracted. (*To* MRS DIGGERTY) Come to me. Now. Now.

MRS DIGGERTY   But your attire, Count — can your passion be sincere?

MUSHROOM   Dear creature, do but lay your hand upon my heart — here — here — here — feel what an alarm of love and gratitude it beats. Now, madam, let's retire to your chamber. We may be interrupted here.

KATTY   (*Off*) You can't speak to her now, sir.

O'DOHERTY   (*Off*) Why not?

MRS DIGGERTY   It's Mirragh — O'Duggerty — O'Murragh — O'Diggerty!

MUSHROOM   Oh God!

KATTY   Because she is ill, sir.

O'DOHERTY   All the more reason I must see her.

MRS DIGGERTY Oh, Mr Soufflé, I am deeply compromised.
MUSHROOM Mr Who?

>KATTY *runs on.*

KATTY Madam, run down the back stairs! Quick!
MRS DIGGERTY *Adieu*, my dear.
KATTY Run! Run!

>MRS DIGGERTY *hoists up her skirts and runs off.*
>MUSHROOM *hoists up his skirts and is about to*
>*follow.*

MUSHROOM I'm going, too.

>KATTY *catches the tail of his dress and holds him*
>*back.*

KATTY Oh, no, you're not, sir.
MUSHROOM Let go of me, Mrs Katty.
KATTY Hold on a second, sir.
MUSHROOM Let me go, Katty.
KATTY You're safer here, sir.
MUSHROOM What are you doing, woman?
KATTY Protecting you, sir.
MUSHROOM Katty, please — !
KATTY You and your lady mustn't be seen together.
MUSHROOM Excellent thinking!
KATTY Leave it all to me. You stay here. I'll put out the candles. (*She does*) He will take you for my mistress.
MUSHROOM But if he —
KATTY Pretend to be very ill. Mimic a fine lady that has the vapours or the cholic.
MUSHROOM Oh my God — !

>*Enter* O'DOHERTY *with a pistol.*

O'DOHERTY Ah! You're in the dark, my dear. Why is that?
KATTY My mistress is very ill and cannot bear the

light.

O'DOHERTY What's her complaint?

MUSHROOM ⎫The cholic.

KATTY ⎭The vapours.

O'DOHERTY There's no cure in the dark, Katty. Light the candles.

MUSHROOM No, no, no candles. No lights, dear, please. No lights.

KATTY She has a headache as well as the vapours —

MUSHROOM And the cholic.

KATTY And lights increase the headache and the cholic —

MUSHROOM And the vapours.

KATTY Let her sit in the dark and she'll be well soon. Are you feeling better now, madam?

MUSHROOM A great deal. But no lights, please, no lights, no lights.

O'DOHERTY (*Softly*) If you prefer no lights, my sweet, then you will have no lights.

MUSHROOM Thank you, my dear.

O'DOHERTY Leave us, Katty. I have some special business with your mistress.

MUSHROOM Special business?

O'DOHERTY Very intimate business, my soul.

MUSHROOM Don't leave, Katty! I have the cholic, sir. And the vapours, sir. And, sir, *I have a very bad headache.* (*As* KATTY *leaves*) Katt-eeeee!

O'DOHERTY Now, my dear, I want to talk to you about something that has given me utmost unease, nay indeed the utmost torture of my mind. My dear, I am jealous.

MUSHROOM Jealous?

O'DOHERTY As are half the husbands of the town; and all occasioned by one man — that coxcomb Mushroom.

MUSHROOM He is a very great coxcomb indeed.

O'DOHERTY And a great jackanapes.

MUSHROOM A huge jackanapes, my dear; an enormous jackanapes.

O'DOHERTY And a popinjay?

MUSHROOM Mushroom? A popinjay and a mountebank.

O'DOHERTY And a poltroon?

MUSHROOM And a varlet and a malapert and a macaroni. Oh, what a macaroni!

O'DOHERTY (*To audience*) In other words — a fop, a dandy.

MUSHROOM Mushroom the Macaroni!

O'DOHERTY That's good. And a libertine, would you say?

MUSHROOM Indeed I would say a libertine — and a charlatan — and the cholic and the vapours and a headache! Oh, how I despise the man!

O'DOHERTY Do you, my dear?

MUSHROOM Thoroughly — without qualification!

O'DOHERTY Though I must own the fellow has something genteel in him.

MUSHROOM Oh, yes, my dear, he is a very *pretty* fellow — that all the world allows.

O'DOHERTY But his prettiness will be his ruin.

MUSHROOM Will it?

O'DOHERTY For as he makes it his business and his boast to win the affection of women everywhere he goes, and as he has made conquests of several married women in this town —

MUSHROOM Mere gossip, my dear. (*To audience*) They always blab, the bitches!

O'DOHERTY — there are half a dozen husbands of us that have agreed —

MUSHROOM *waits.* O'DOHERTY *does not speak.*

MUSHROOM Agreed?

O'DOHERTY To poison him.

MUSHROOM Poison! But that will be murder, my dear.

O'DOHERTY It will. But before we get to that, one of our company has vowed that if Mushroom ever enters his house again he will put ten inches of cold iron into the rascal's bowels.

MUSHROOM Bowels?

O'DOHERTY Can you imagine?

MUSHROOM I can — I can — Oh God I can!

O'DOHERTY As for you, my dear, if I ever catch the fellow

	ogling you, following you around —
MUSHROOM	An old bat like me?
O'DOHERTY	— even smiling at you, I will put the lining of this little pistol into the very middle of his skull.
MUSHROOM	Oh-oh-oh!
O'DOHERTY	Why are you all in a tremor, my soul?
MUSHROOM	I am ill, dear sir —
O'DOHERTY	You have the shaking ague. You are all in a cold sweat.
MUSHROOM	— mighty, mighty ill, sir.
O'DOHERTY	Indeed you are. (*Calls*) Katty! Katty! You must have help immediately.

KATTY enters.

O'DOHERTY	Send for Mr Carnage, the surgeon. He must bleed my wife at once.
KATTY	Yes, sir.
MUSHROOM	Oooooh.
O'DOHERTY	And fetch Dr Fillgrave, too. Tell him my wife is very ill and must be blistered.

KATTY exits.

MUSHROOM	I'm feeling better already. (*To audience*) What the hell shall I do? I'll certainly be discovered now!
O'DOHERTY	How are you now, my dear?
MUSHROOM	Oh better, better, a great deal.
O'DOHERTY	Splendid. I'll have you bled plentifully and ten good rousing blisters laid on by way of prevention. Just sit still and rest until the medical men come. (*To audience*) When I'm finished with him he'll be cured forever of trespassing upon matrimonial premises.

He exits.

MUSHROOM	(*To audience*) Oh God, I wish I were out of this

damned country! I've often heard of the wild Irish but never believed it until now! Savages! Barbarians! Poison a man for merely having an intrigue with his wife! We never mind such things in England.

Enter KATTY *and* MRS DIGGERTY *with candles.*

MUSHROOM	No lights, please, no lights, no lights!
KATTY	It's only me, sir, and Mrs Diggerty.
MUSHROOM	If you don't get me out of this damned house, madam, I am a dead man.
MRS DIGGERTY	I'm distracted — I can't think — my husband suspects I'm —
MUSHROOM	He may suspect you. He's going to shoot *me*! Help me!
MRS DIGGERTY	Tell him — tell him you came here in that disguise — just to give him a laugh.
MUSHROOM	'Just to give him a — '!The woman's an idiot! Mrs Katty, help me, please! I have got to get out of this place — now!
KATTY	The portmanteau trunk. You might be able to fit into it.
MUSHROOM	Anything — anything — dear Mrs Katty. My life is in your hands.

KATTY *has now pulled on stage a trunk which she opens.*

MUSHROOM	If I escape from this damned country, my dear, I promise you you'll never see — Excellent, Mrs Katty. The very thing.
KATTY	Get in. Hurry up. My master's coming.
MUSHROOM	Will I fit?
KATTY	Quick! Quick!

The trunk is on its end so that when MUSHROOM *gets into it he is upright. The door is ajar.*

MUSHROOM	Put in my clothes — there — cram me in —

buckle me up — will I have enough air? Very well, excellent well, Mrs Katty — it will do — snug, snug, damned snug —

Enter O'DOHERTY; *in his hand a naked sword.*

O'DOHERTY What are you doing with that portmanteau?
KATTY Nothing, sir. We're just —
O'DOHERTY What have you got in there?
MRS DIGGERTY It's only a —

O'DOHERTY *is about to plunge his sword into the trunk.*

O'DOHERTY Speak this minute or I'll put my sword up to the hilt in it.
MUSHROOM Hold, hold, my dear Diggerty!
O'DOHERTY Who's that?

Enter HAMILTON.

MUSHROOM It's I! It's I!
O'DOHERTY Who is 'I'?
MUSHROOM It's Mushroom. Your friend, Mushroom.
HAMILTON What's the coxcomb up to now?
MUSHROOM (*Peeping out the door*) It's the count — your friend, the count.
O'DOHERTY The count, indeed. Or is it the countess?
HAMILTON Is he going on his holidays?
MUSHROOM I can explain everything, Diggerty.

O'DOHERTY *shuts the trunk.*

O'DOHERTY I'm sure you can, Mushroom. And I'll give you every opportunity. For we have invited half the town in tonight and they all want a peep at you. Give me a hand here. He's got to be transported downstairs to greet our guests. That's it.

One end of the trunk is lifted — and dropped.
Another end is lifted (so that MUSHROOM *is now*
upside down) — and dropped. The trunk is
stood on its end — and tipped over. Throughout
all this MUSHROOM *squeals in terror —* 'Help!
Help! Let me out! I'm suffocating! You're
killing me! Help! Help!' *Eventually* KATTY
and HAMILTON *and* MRS DIGGERTY *drag the*
trunk off. As they do —

O'DOHERTY Careful, there. That's a valuable parcel. And
we've got to keep him healthy at least for a few
more hours. (*To audience*) And that's the end of
our story: How Count Mushroom made
himself an object for a farce. But then if every
fine lady and every coxcomb in this town were
turned into a farce, we'd be the merriest
people in all Europe. But ours is over for
tonight.
Indeed I think it's fairly ended.
The coxcomb's punished;
The fine Irish lady's mended.

Suddenly MRS DIGGERTY's *head appears round*
the door.

MRS DIGGERTY (*Winking broadly at the audience*) For the time
being!